RACIAL LITERACY

Recognizing Microaggressions

Nadra Nittle

Enslow Publishing

101 W. 23rd Street
Suite 240
New York, NY 10011
USA

enslow.com

Published in 2019 by Enslow Publishing, LLC.
101 W. 23rd Street, Suite 240, New York, NY 10011

Library of Congress Cataloging-in-Publication Data

Name: Nittle, Nadra, author.
Title: Recognizing microaggressions / Nadra Nittle.
Description: New York : Enslow Publishing, [2019] | Series: Racial literacy |
    Audience: Grade level 7–12. | Includes bibliographical references and index.
Identifiers: LCCN 2018019105| ISBN 9781978504660 (library bound) | ISBN
    9781978505612 (pbk.)
Subjects: LCSH: Microaggressions. | Prejudices. | Discrimination.
Classification: LCC BF575.P9 N58 2019 | DDC 303.3/85–dc23
LC record available at https://lccn.loc.gov/2018019105

Printed in the United States of America

To Our Readers: We have done our best to make sure all website addresses in this
book were active and appropriate when we went to press. However, the author
and the publisher have no control over and assume no liability for the material
available on those websites or on any websites they may link to. Any comments or
suggestions can be sent by email to customerservice@enslow.com.

CONTENTS

Introduction

If you've ever had the nagging feeling that someone was racist but you couldn't prove it, you're far from alone. It's a common experience for people of color. Thankfully, society has started to take these experiences more seriously.

Perhaps a waiter gave your family poor service in a restaurant while showering the other diners with attention. Maybe you're one of the few students of color at your school, and your teacher never seems to notice your raised hand. Or your peers can freely share complaints or question authority, while you're called "aggressive" or a "troublemaker" for doing the same. These examples are all based on real-life experiences that members of racial minority groups have had. Scholars have a name for them: microaggressions.

This form of subtle racism may not seem very alarming, but it can have terrible consequences. It can affect a person's health, leading to problems like high blood pressure, anxiety, or depression. It can affect

Even very young children of color may be on the receiving end of racial microaggressions. Both classmates and teachers may treat them differently.

people's treatment in schools, workplaces, hospitals, shopping centers, entertainment venues, and their own neighborhoods. It can cause a seemingly minor situation to quickly spiral out of control. In short, microaggressions matter.

Every day, people of color all over the world face this form of subtle racism. Over time, microaggressions take a toll on one's mental health and cause race relations to worsen. But microaggressions can be difficult to remedy because most people responsible for these behaviors insist they're not racist and have done nothing wrong. On the other hand, victims of these behaviors may try to ignore them because they've been told they're no big deal. They may reason that it's not as if someone beat them up because of their race, painted racist graffiti, or outright admitted to being racist. But this way of thinking let's people who commit microaggressions off the hook for the dozens of small ways they make life difficult for racial minorities. If racism is ever to end, it must be addressed

Racial microaggressions can take a toll on a person's mental health. Depression and anxiety can develop in individuals subjected to subtle racism.

at both the macro (large) and micro (small) level. All too often, society prefers to focus on macro racism while dismissing the microaggressions that occur day in and day out.

Most people of color will not be victims of hate crimes. They will not be killed by police. They will not be openly told that they are being treated differently because of their skin color. But they will experience microaggressions.

In this book, you'll learn the definition and history of microaggressions. You'll read examples of microaggressions in a variety of settings—from college campuses to clothing stores. Most important, you'll learn ways to protect and stand up for yourself.

Sadly, it's nearly impossible to avoid racism if you're a person of color. But you don't have to bury your feelings and stay silent when microaggressions occur. In many cases, you don't have to attend schools, support businesses, or live in places that expose you to these behaviors either. Fighting back against microaggressions is an important way to stop them from overwhelming you.

CHAPTER 1

Just What Are Microaggressions?

"Racial microaggression" is a complex term for a concept that's actually quite simple. Think of it as racism with a little "R." It's used to describe the commonplace forms of racism that millions of people face every day at school, work, or merely going about their day. When racism trends on social media or makes news headlines, it usually involves capital "R" racism. A deadly police shooting of an unarmed person of color. A hate crime. A racial discrimination lawsuit against a company with unfair hiring practices.

Microaggressions aren't so dramatic. They're the subtle slights based on skin color that people might keep to themselves, only discuss with family or friends, or shrug off entirely. But this form of racism matters just as much as the blatant form that makes the news. That's because over time, microaggressions can have a serious impact on one's mental and physical health.

The expression "death by a thousand paper cuts" refers to the devastation that a series of small, unfortunate events can have on a person. Microaggressions are the paper cuts of racism. When one is exposed to several over a long stretch of time, the effect can be dangerous.

Before delving into just why microaggressions are so troubling and what to do about them, it's important to know the history of the term. Let's explore.

The Origin of the Term

In the 1970s, Dr. Chester Pierce, then a psychiatry professor at Harvard University Medical School, first coined the term "racial microaggressions."[1] The concept also can be found in the work of psychology professors Jack Dovidio of Yale University and Samuel Gaertner of the University of Delaware.[2] Dovidio and Gaertner's research suggests that even whites who believe in racial equality may unknowingly behave in ways that show racial bias, or favoritism. Psychologist Claude Steele's research explored the issue, finding that Blacks and women (of any race) do worse on standardized tests when exposed to stereotypes about race and gender.[3] But it is Derald Wing Sue, a Columbia University psychologist, who made the concept of racial microaggressions really popular. His 2007 research paper in *American Psychologist* about the topic, "Racial Microaggressions in Everyday Life: Implications for Clinical Practice,"[4] is thought to have made this issue mainstream and given researchers a clear way to study it.

Writing for *Psychology Today* in 2010, Sue defined racial microaggressions as follows:

Racial microaggressions are the brief and everyday slights, insults, indignities and denigrating messages sent to people of color by well-intentioned white people who are unaware of the hidden messages being communicated. These messages may be sent verbally ("You speak good English."), nonverbally (clutching one's purse more tightly) or environmentally (symbols like the confederate flag or using American Indian mascots).[5]

In his groundbreaking paper in *American Psychologist*, Sue divided racial microaggressions into three categories: microassaults, microinsults, and microinvalidations. Quite the mouthful, huh? But these concepts are really not hard to grasp.

The late Dr. Chester Pierce coined the term "microaggression" in the 1970s. He was subjected to both overt and covert racism himself.

Microassaults involve deliberate acts of harm against members of a minority group, such as a shopkeeper intentionally waiting on them last. Microinsults are spoken (or unspoken) insults, such as asking a student of color how they managed to get into a top college. The insult suggests that the student won admission only because of an affirmative action program and not because of their hard work, discipline, or smarts. Finally, microinvalidations overlook the experiences of people of color. Asking someone of Asian descent where she's really from is an example because the question ignores that Asian Americans exist and have for generations. A microinvalidation can involve a white person denying the feelings people of color have about race. Telling a Latino man "It's all in your head" when he says he lost a job because of his skin color is an example.

A Personal Connection

The research of Chester Pierce and Derald Wing Sue has helped countless people learn about microaggressions. The public also can learn about race relations by looking at the

A woman wearing a hijab, or head covering, may face all sorts of microaggressions related to her religious background—from subtle slights to outright insults.

lives of these professors. Both men experienced racism in some form.

Born in 1927, Dr. Chester Pierce experienced overt forms of discrimination. He was reportedly the first Black student to play a football game in the South on a racially integrated football team. However, he could not stay in the same hotel as his Harvard teammates when the school played the University of Virginia in 1947.[6] Jim Crow, a set of laws that made separation of the races a way of life, kept Black Americans out of hotels, restaurants, schools, and many other places through the mid-twentieth century. So, Dr. Pierce was not only familiar with microaggressions but also racism at its most fierce.

Dr. Pierce grew up during a time when the US was racially segregated. This "white only" sign, from a Mississippi bus station, shows how racism was enforced in public accommodations.

Dr. Chester Pierce: A Pioneer

Dr. Chester Pierce was born March 4 1927, in New York.[7] He earned a medical degree from Harvard in 1952. As a student, Pierce played football, basketball, and lacrosse.

He spent much of his career at Massachusetts General Hospital, where since 2009 the division of global psychiatry has borne his name. He presided over a number of organizations, including the American Board of Psychiatry and Neurology. He was founding president of the Psychiatrists of America Association and a consultant for the children's show *Sesame Street*.

He published more than 180 books and papers on race, extreme environments, sports medicine, and more. His work took him to all seven continents, and a peak in Antarctica is named after him.

He died September 23, 2016.

An Asian American, Sue has shared his experiences with microaggressions. In *Psychology Today*, he recalled the time when he and a Black coworker took an early-morning flight with few passengers.[8] At first, the flight attendant told them to sit anywhere they wanted, so they sat across the aisle from each other in the front of the plane. Just before the plane took off, three white men boarded. They took seats in front of Sue and his coworker. Rather than ask the group of white men to change seats, the white flight attendant asked Sue and his colleague to move to the back of the plane to keep its weight balanced.

Sue and his coworker took offense, but the flight attendant denied asking them to move because of their race. She told them they were being "too sensitive" and that she did not see "color." She explained that she just wanted everyone to have a safe flight. She then shut down the discussion.

"Were we being overly sensitive, or was the flight attendant being racist?" Sue wondered. "That is a question that people of color are constantly faced with in their day-to-day interactions with well-intentioned white folks who experience themselves as good, moral, and decent human beings."[9]

Sue and his Black colleague considered it a microaggression when the flight attendant asked them to move after a group of white men boarded the plane, but she denied racism played a role in her request. Do you agree?

Racial microaggressions are tricky because one never knows for sure why people behave the way they do. It doesn't help matters that most people responsible for microaggressions don't willingly admit to wrongdoing. Imagine if the flight attendant had told Sue, "I'm sorry. I didn't mean to treat you unfairly. Why don't you stay put, and I'll ask these other gentlemen to go to the back. After all, you were here first." This would have cleared the tension in the air and made Sue and his colleague feel like valued customers. Unfortunately, whites all too often deny any responsibility for their racism. This leads people of color to feel hurt, angry, or disrespected.

The Case Against Microaggressions

Not everyone agrees that whites need to own up to microaggressions, or that the idea is a valid one. Critics of the microaggressions concept say it leads people of color to have a "victim mentality." Kenneth R. Thomas, formerly a psychology professor at the University of Wisconsin-Madison, criticized Sue's work in a letter to *American Psychologist*.

"The theory, in general, characterizes people of color as weak and vulnerable, and reinforces a culture of victimization instead of a culture of opportunity," he wrote.[10]

Pierce and Sue, the champions of the microaggressions concept, did not behave like victims in life. Pierce, especially, had to overcome a great deal of bias to get into Harvard and become a star psychiatrist. Pointing out that racial slights exist does not lead to a victim mentality any more than noting that full-blown racism exists. It's simply a way of

It can be uncomfortable to speak up when someone behaves offensively, but discussing the issue may make you feel better.

accepting reality and pinpointing the behaviors that people of color deal with regularly.

Thomas isn't the only microaggressions critic, however. Columbia University linguistics professor John McWhorter warned against describing every off-color remark as a microaggression. He told the *New York Times* that he thinks it's abusive to assume that a Black student got into a top college because of affirmative action. Yet, he doesn't think it's offensive, or a microinvalidation, when whites claim not to see race. "I think that's taking it too far," he said.[11]

The disagreements scholars have about microaggressions aren't likely to end anytime soon, if ever. That means it's really your call to decide what you consider a microaggression. If you feel like you're being treated differently because of your race, ethnicity, or a similar reason, you likely are. If someone you have to interact with regularly has done something to offend you, continue to observe the person's behavior. If you notice a pattern, don't shy away from calling it like you see it. That doesn't mean you have to confront the person. It just means you can put a name on the behavior that's troubling you. Doing so won't make you a victim but can give you a greater sense of control the next time you run into such behavior.

CHAPTER 2

Why Microaggressions Matter

Compared to problems like police brutality or housing discrimination, microaggressions may not seem very important. In fact, it's tempting to dismiss them altogether because they're seemingly not a life-or-death issue. While it definitely doesn't feel good to be slighted based on skin color, it's really no big deal, right? Can't a person just shake it off and move on with life? Not quite. That's because in certain situations and settings, racial microaggressions may have serious consequences.

Trayvon Martin's tragic 2012 killing is a case in point. One can argue that the teenager was simply in the wrong place at the wrong time. But had Trayvon not been African American, it's very likely he would still be alive today. Consider the role that racial microaggressions played in his final moments.

A Suspicious Person

On February 26, 2012, a neighborhood watchman named George Zimmerman phoned police to report a "suspicious" person he'd seen in his gated community in Sanford, Florida. Zimmerman hadn't caught the person in the act of doing anything. He hadn't seen him vandalizing property, stealing, or harming himself or anyone else. Still, Zimmerman was convinced: The person was dangerous. Here's what he told police about this individual:[1]

"Hey, we've had some break-ins in my neighborhood, and there's a real suspicious guy...," Zimmerman said. "This guy looks like he's up to no good, or he's on drugs or something. It's raining and he's just walking around, looking about."

Of course, the person Zimmerman described to the police dispatcher was Trayvon Martin. Trayvon was a seventeen-year-old visiting his father, a resident of the gated community. Zimmerman's decision to call the police on him for "walking around, looking about" is like the microaggression of purse clutching on steroids. What about Trayvon's behavior required police attention? Even Zimmerman's mention of break-ins makes little sense because he hadn't witnessed Trayvon committing a burglary. Since the person responsible for the break-ins had apparently not been caught, Zimmerman had no reason to link the teen to those crimes. He didn't know what race, gender, or age the burglars were. So he had no reason to suspect Trayvon was involved.

Zimmerman also gave no real reason as to why he thought Trayvon was on drugs. He simply set eyes on the Black teen and decided he was "up to no good." Judging someone of

A protester holds up a sign featuring a photograph of Trayvon Martin, the teen fatally shot by a neighborhood watchman who thought he looked suspicious.

a different race based on stereotypes is known as racial prejudice. Since Zimmerman knew nothing about Trayvon Martin and hadn't seen him do anything illegal, it's safe to say that he prejudged the teen. Had Trayvon been white, there's a good chance Zimmerman would've reacted completely different. He may have seen him wandering around and figured he was lost, or just a spacey kid. The thought that a white teen walking in the rain must be a burglar or high on drugs probably would not have entered his head.

If Trayvon had survived his encounter with George Zimmerman, he would've experienced it as a microaggression. Say Zimmerman, as the 9-1-1 dispatcher instructed,[2] had stopped following him and the police had driven to the housing complex and approached the teen. Trayvon likely would've been amazed that someone had reported him to the police. After all, he had just been walking back to his father's home after a short trip to the store.[3] The idea that someone thought he was a burglar may have hurt or offended him, or he may have chalked it up to being a young Black man in America. In other words, whether or not he knew the term "racial microaggression," he may have viewed the experience as just another of the many indignities, or humiliations, that people of color suffer all the time because of racism.

But Trayvon did not live to tell his story. Against the dispatcher's advice, Zimmerman pursued the teen, and they began to fight. Zimmerman eventually pulled out a gun and fatally shot Trayvon Martin. Using Florida's controversial Stand Your Ground law, a jury acquitted Zimmerman of murder on July 13, 2013.[4] The law permits people to use deadly force and not retreat if they believe they're in a life-threatening situation or at risk of serious harm.[5] Zimmerman said he believed Trayvon would kill him during their fight. Since then, Zimmerman has been involved in several violent incidents. He's continued a pattern of behavior he'd shown even before killing Trayvon Martin.[6]

African Americans complain that white women hold their purses tighter when a Black person passes, as if all Blacks are thieves.

Trayvon's Life Mattered

Trayvon Benjamin Martin was born February 5, 1995, in Florida to Sybrina Fulton and Tracy Martin. He had an older brother, Jhavaris Fulton.

Trayvon celebrated his seventeenth birthday shortly before his death. He'd received Levi's, Adidas, and cologne as gifts.[7] He'd also been looking forward to prom. He was a student at Dr. Michael M. Krop Senior High School in Miami.

At 6-feet-3, he was just 140 pounds,[8] thin for his height. His nickname, "Slimm," fit him perfectly.

Trayvon was considering an aviation career and hoped to attend Florida A&M University.

His killing led to nationwide protests, and Black Lives Matter cofounder Patrisse Cullors said it marked an "urgency to fight for black lives."[9]

In 2012, the Trayvon Martin Foundation launched. It fights gun violence.

Microaggressions and Our Health

George Zimmerman's senseless killing of Trayvon Martin shows how a microaggression can quickly balloon into a deadly encounter. That situation is far from the only kind in which microaggressions have life-or-death consequences. Microaggressions occur in health care settings all the time. There, they put people of color's lives at risk. Even babies and children of color aren't spared from microaggressions in hospitals.

A 2017 Stanford University study found racial disparities, or differences, in the care that babies in California's neonatal intensive care units (NICUs) receive. Overall, white babies received better care than Black or Hispanic babies, the study found. While research did not uncover any clear signs of biased treatment, the senior author of the study suggested that microaggressions might be a factor.

"Unconscious social biases that we all have can make their way into the NICU," said Dr. Jochen Profit, a Stanford pediatrics professor. "We would like to encourage NICU caregivers to think about how these disparities play out in their own units and how they can be reduced."[10]

An alarming study by Stanford University researchers found that even newborn babies of color may be the targets of microaggressions, as white babies appear to receive better care.

The study examined 18,616 babies with weights under 3.3 pounds. The researchers reviewed whether the babies received standard medical care. This care includes screenings for eye diseases or steroids before birth to help their lungs develop. They also found out whether the babies caught infections in the hospital and how well they grew. Across the board, the white babies had the edge.

Premature babies need all the help they can get to survive, so the idea that microaggressions may affect their treatment is extremely alarming. It also shows just how deep racism runs, even in a supposedly "liberal" state like California. If the color of a newborn's skin influences medical treatment, it doesn't bode well for people of color generally in health care settings. While George Zimmerman painted teenage Trayvon Martin as a scary Black man to justify killing him, there's absolutely no explanation that a health care provider can give to excuse why white babies in their units get better care than infants of color. They can deny treating any baby differently but must be held accountable when the data reveals otherwise.

Unfortunately, the Stanford study isn't the only one to find that microaggressions affect the health care of the youngest people of color. A 2012 University of Washington study found that pediatricians with racial biases were more likely to give Black children ibuprofen than powerful pain medication. Other studies have found that doctors fail to manage the pain of Black children with sickle cell anemia.[11]

Given these findings, there's no doubt that the public should be as concerned about microaggressions as they are

Black children aren't as likely to receive strong pain medication for their health problems as white children are. This signals that microaggressions are a real problem in medicine.

about the overt racism covered by the news. Lives depend on a solution to this widespread problem. This is not only because vigilantes, like Zimmerman, or health care providers have racial biases. It's also because of the impact that subtle racism has on a person's health outside a medical setting.

According to the American Psychiatric Association (APA), microaggressions can lead to mental health problems, such as depression and anxiety, or physical problems like pain and fatigue. Microaggressions are so harmful that simply thinking about them can produce a negative physical response.

"Just the anticipation of experiencing racial discrimination can be enough to cause a significant spike in stress responses," the APA points out. "A study showed that Latina students who interacted with a person with presumably racist ideas showed an increased 'fight or flight' response with higher blood pressure and faster heart rates."[12]

The APA even issued a resolution against racism. It stated how important it is for health care providers to consider the role racism plays in patients' lives.

Now that you know how serious microaggressions are, treat them accordingly. Don't shrug them off and, if you can, limit your dealings with people who've exposed you to such behavior. Your quality of life matters.

CHAPTER 3

The Soft Bigotry of Low Expectations

When President Barack Obama spoke at Morehouse College's 2013 graduation ceremony, he mentioned that many Black children receive the same advice from their elders. If you're an African American, or belong to another minority group, you've likely heard this tip before.

"Every one of you have a grandma or an uncle or a parent who's told you that at some point in life, as an African American, you have to work twice as hard as anyone else if you want to get by," Obama said.[1]

Why do so many people of color tell youth that they have to put in double the effort to get ahead? They know that racism is so widespread that even the youngest children can't avoid it. As early as preschool, Black and Brown children may be disciplined more harshly than their white peers for similar behavior. They also face doubts about their intelligence, not to

Children of color face a number of barriers in the classroom, including doubts about their intelligence and harsher forms of school discipline.

mention textbooks that present a lopsided view of history. In college, the challenges that students of color face may get even harder.

If only students could get an education without encountering overt racism or racial microaggressions. While that day may never come, steps have been taken to address inequities in the classroom.

The Problem with School Discipline

If you've ever spent time with a preschooler, you know that they're really cute but not always easy to handle. They make messes, throw temper tantrums, and have a hard time sitting still. No matter their color or country of origin, children who've yet to hit kindergarten tend to act out in these ways. But in the United States, Black children are the preschoolers most likely to be kicked out of school for misbehaving.

On each school day in 2016, about 250 preschoolers in the United States were suspended or expelled, according to a Center for American Progress (CAP) report.[2] Black children, especially boys, were 2.2 times more likely to be pushed out of preschool than their peers. CAP policy analyst Rashid Malik

Research has found that teachers have racial bias, especially against the Black boys in their classes. Black boys receive the harshest forms of punishment in school, even when they have done nothing wrong.

suggested that the implicit biases of preschool teachers might be to blame for many Black tots being punished so severely. Implicit biases lead to microaggressions. Malik described them as "automatic and unconscious stereotypes that influence judgments and decisions regarding others."[3]

He pointed to the Yale Child Study Center to make his point.[4] It showed that teachers asked to watch a video to identify problem student behavior paid closer attention to Black boys. They noted their behavior as troublesome. None of the children filmed had actually behaved inappropriately. That the teachers made this mistake shows that they might unfairly punish Black boys in their own classrooms.

Because of such research, politicians in states such as Maryland, Ohio, and Colorado are trying to pass laws that would ban suspensions of nonviolent preschoolers. These laws would not apply to students of all ages, so they don't address the fact that throughout grades K–12, Black children are most often suspended or expelled. In fact, Black students are three times more likely to be suspended and expelled than white students.[5] Many times, these suspensions are related to gray-area offenses, such as talking back or not following instructions. As a result, the Los Angeles Unified School District announced in 2013 that it would stop suspending students for what it calls "willful defiance."[6] Several other school districts have followed suit.

Reducing suspensions at all grade levels is an important step. There's no question that racial microaggressions exist and that African American boys are the most affected. A 2016 *Psychological Science* study found that whites view Black

Black boys are often pushed out of school because of unfair discipline policies. Black girls also face harsh forms of punishment in school even when playing innocently with their classmates.

boys as young as five years old as violent, dangerous, hostile, and aggressive.[7] This might also explain why the preschool teachers watching the Yale video mistakenly identified the Black boys' behavior as a problem when it was not.

Punishing Black boys without a valid reason has real-world consequences. Suspended children are more likely to drop out of school and be swept into the criminal justice system. But lowering the number of student suspensions is not enough. Teachers and administrators need implicit bias training to help them recognize whether they may be unconsciously acting in ways that harm students. Teacher biases not only influence which students get disciplined

Implicit Bias Testing

The Implicit Association Test (IAT) uses words and images to uncover the hidden biases people have. In 1998, Yale University freshmen became the first group to take the test. The results proved shocking.

"They were confused, they were irritated, they were thoughtful and challenged, and they formed groups to discuss it," recalled psychologist Mahzarin Banaji.[8]

As time has passed, the IAT has faced criticism for not meeting scientific standards. For example, those who retake the test may get very different results. Other critics say the test doesn't hold people responsible for their views because it finds prejudice in almost everyone. However, the IAT has led many organizations to get members to take a hard look at their racial attitudes.

but also which students excel in class. While implicit bias testing may be imperfect, training people to spot racism and take action against it helps institutions to take prejudice seriously.

Teachers Make a Difference

Students of color face microaggressions about their behavior and their intellect. All too often, Black and Brown children have to prove that they're just as intelligent as their white and Asian American peers. A 2016 American Educational Research Association (AERA) report found that Black and Hispanic third graders are about half as likely as whites to take part in gifted and talented (GATE) programs.[9] So, why might this signal subtle racism? The researchers found that even when white and Black children scored the same on math and reading tests, white children were still twice as likely as Blacks to be placed in GATE classes. That's not all. When students have teachers of color, Black children are just as likely to be identified as gifted as whites. In other words, because teachers of color lack the racial biases of white teachers, they're better able to spot giftedness in Black children.

White teachers are more likely to recommend children of color for special education classes than for gifted classes. But teachers of color are more likely to see these students as gifted and talented.

The AERA findings show that teacher perception plays a huge role in which children are labeled gifted. This is why a Broward County, Florida, school district changed how it screened children for giftedness.[10] The district had all second graders take a nonverbal screening test. Students who scored high on this test went on to take an IQ test. Previously, either teachers or parents referred students to take such tests. By screening all children, the district sidestepped the racial biases of teachers and tripled the number of Black and Hispanic students in GATE classes.

One might say gifted children of color overlooked in favor of white children were victims of the "soft bigotry of low expectations." In 1999, when George W. Bush was Texas governor, he used this phrase during a speech about improving education policy.

> No child in America should be segregated by low expectations, imprisoned by illiteracy, abandoned to frustration and darkness of self-doubt. ...," he said. "Now some say it is unfair to hold disadvantaged children to rigorous standards. I say it is discrimination to require anything less—the soft bigotry of low expectations.[11]

Bush's speechwriter Michael Gerson coined the phrase "soft bigotry of low expectations" to describe the lower standards that schools often set for disadvantaged children. Critics of Bush's education policies, such as No Child Left Behind, certainly did not think that disadvantaged children should be held to lower academic standards. They did point out, though, that schools needed more resources to ensure that all children receive the education they deserve.

Microaggressions on Campus

College is an exciting time. It's a place where you can meet lifelong friends, prepare for a career, and live independently for the first time. But for many young people of color at predominantly white institutions, college is also a place where both racial microaggressions and blatant racism are real problems. For students who come from communities of color, encountering racist roommates, faculty, or officials can be unsettling. Being the victim of a hate crime or living on a campus where students host racist parties can be devastating.

The year 2017 saw a slew of racist incidents take place on college campuses. At Cornell University, a group

Students of color may face various microaggressions on college campuses—from racist parties to classmates who believe they got into college only because of affirmative action.

of fraternity members beat up a Black student and called him racial slurs. Black students on campus protested on the victim's behalf. That same year, anti-Black graffiti was left on the campuses of universities including Southern Illinois University–Edwardsville, Drake University, Cabrini University, University of Michigan, and Westfield State University. Also, fliers from white supremacist groups were found on the campuses of the University of Louisville, Purdue, and Stockton universities.[12]

At the University of Hartford in Connecticut, a white student was arrested after smearing her bodily fluids on her Black roommate's belongings.[13] She also called her roommate "Jamaican Barbie" behind her back. The Black student likely sensed she was in a hostile environment but had no way to prove it. After bragging about her misdeeds to her friends, the white student's horrible behavior was discovered.

The above incidents all fall into the category that Derald Wing Sue called racial microassaults, or acts of deliberate harm against people of color.

Why did so many racist incidents on college campuses make headlines in 2017? Some activists point to the Trump effect, arguing that the election of a man who often used racial stereotypes on the campaign trail gave racists the boldness to act out.

But even when Barack Obama was president, racism thrived on college campuses. In 2015, protests broke out at the University of Missouri after students accused campus officials of ignoring acts of racial bigotry.[14] This inspired

Asian Americans may be well represented on college campuses, but that doesn't mean they don't face racism at universities. A UCLA student revealed how resentful some white students are of their Asian peers when her racist rant went viral.

college students on other campuses to protest racism at their universities too. In addition, college parties with racist themes, such as the "Compton Cookout" or "Cowboys and Indians," sparked controversy throughout Obama's time in office.

For every racist incident on a college campus that makes news headlines, there are dozens that don't. News crews don't show up when students of color are asked to show their IDs to prove they're really enrolled at a university. They're not around when classmates assume that Black or Brown students only got into college because of affirmative action.

Reporters typically don't come running when students complain that too many Asian Americans attend a university. The exception occurred in 2011, after a white UCLA student recorded a rant about all of the "Asians in the library."[15] The video rant went viral, and the student's racism was harshly criticized. If she hadn't made the unwise decision to record her racist views, her Asian American classmates wouldn't have learned how she really felt about them.

Unfortunately, if you're a student from a minority group attending a predominantly white institution, it's impossible to avoid microaggressions. But you can try to lower the chances that you'll be affected by subtle racism. Before you decide on a college, know that the environment of a university matters just as much as its academic reputation. In other words, just because a university is highly regarded doesn't mean it's the school for you. Question if this institution has made any real commitment to diversity. You'll likely have an easier transition to college if you choose one that has a multicultural agenda. This includes clubs, housing, and courses of study related to people of color.

CHAPTER 4

Shopping While Black (or Brown)

There's a reason shopping is nicknamed "retail therapy." It's supposed to be a feel-good activity. But for people of color, shopping and dining out come with microaggressions. They may be followed around in stores, given bad service in restaurants, or harassed by other customers.

Thanks to social media, it's now easier than ever for Black and Brown people to spread the word when a business treats them badly. Sadly, one of the most common experiences that people of color have in such establishments is being treated more like criminals than customers.

Customers, Not Criminals

On January 31, 2018, James Conley III walked into an Iowa Old Navy store wearing a jacket from the brand. When he tried to purchase some hoodies, the staff asked him to remove his jacket so they could scan it as well.

"First, I started laughing because I didn't believe what I was hearing," wrote Conley, an African American, on Facebook.[1] He soon realized the staff thought he was trying to steal his own jacket. They told him it was store policy to scan Old Navy items that customers wear into the store. A frequent customer, Conley said that this had never happened to him before. He also noticed that the staff did not ask to scan the Old Navy gear that white patrons wore.

After scanning his jacket, Old Navy staff tried to make him repay for it, Conley wrote. He made them watch the store's surveillance tape to prove he'd entered wearing the jacket. Conley kept cool throughout the ordeal. He jotted down the names of the staffers involved and filmed them. He then wrote about his experience in a Facebook post shared nearly 160,000 times. After Conley's post went viral, Old Navy apologized and fired the employees who'd treated him so badly.[2]

Unfortunately, what happened to Conley is not unusual. People of color routinely face microaggressions in stores. A 2015 Gallup poll found that more Blacks felt they'd been recently discriminated against while shopping (24 percent) than dealing with police (18 percent).[3] In fact, more Blacks said they'd been discriminated against while shopping than doing any other activity.

Today's technology has given shoppers of color a voice. Recording acts of discrimination on cell phones and posting the footage on social media are important ways to raise awareness about what it's like to shop while Black (or Brown). Most people will not openly admit to treating

Even though Blacks have an estimated buying power of $1.2 trillion, according to Nielsen, they are often treated more like criminals than shoppers in retail establishments.

someone differently because of race. There is an exception, however. When fellow customers are bigots, they may not bother to hide their racism.

The Trump Effect

Make no mistake: racism in the United States existed before Donald Trump was even born, let alone became president. Those who behave as if bigotry is a new problem that surfaced after the 2016 election aren't being honest about American history. That being said, the Southern Poverty Law Center (SPLC) did report a rise in racist incidents following

Trump's election to office. His desire to keep out immigrants by "building the wall" and issuing travel bans have made some bigots feel bold enough to harass people in schools, on the streets, and in stores.

Just a month after the 2016 election, a white woman standing in line at a Kentucky JCPenney yelled out racist comments to a Latina customer in front of her.[4] The white woman grew angry because the woman's friend dropped off another item to buy. But that was no excuse for her racist and xenophobic attack. Xenophobia is the fear or hatred of foreigners.

After Donald Trump won the presidential election in 2016, many Latinx consumers have faced bigotry and xenophobia from white shoppers in retail establishments.

The white woman accused the victim of being on welfare and told her to speak English. She said, "Go back to wherever the f--k you come from, lady."[5]

A bystander took video of the incident and posted it to Facebook. It received more than six million views. The encounter was a preview of the racial tensions to come in Trump's America.

The next several months saw a number of such incidents. In May 2017 alone, three videos of white customers in stores bullying people of color went viral. The words of these bullies constituted microassaults, or behaviors meant to hurt racial minorities.

At a Virginia Trader Joe's, a white customer told a Muslim American shopper, "I wish they didn't let you in the country."[6]

"Excuse me?" the Muslim American woman responded. "I was born here."

The white woman then mentioned that President Obama was no longer in office. She said this meant the White House was now Muslim-free and predicted that Obama would be in jail in the future. Of course, the woman's remarks were untrue. Obama is not a Muslim (though if he were, that would be fine). He wrote much about his Christian faith in his memoir, *Dreams from My Father*, and has commented on it many times since then. Also, there's no reason to believe that he'd ever be imprisoned.

Altogether, the woman's words reveal that she definitely felt a sense of power having Trump as president. After all, she didn't just insult the Muslim American woman but tied her insults to the fact that Obama was out of the White

House. Plus, her comment that the woman had been "let in the country" echoes Trump's xenophobic comments about immigrants. This comment was a microinvalidation as well as a microassault, as it denied the reality that Muslim people are born and raised in the United States.

Later that month, also in Virginia, a white female customer at Sprint called a Hispanic man a racial slur after he tried to help her find another branch of the store. He'd overheard her complaints about the store they were in and interrupted her phone conversation to refer her to a new Sprint site. In return, the woman lashed out racially. After telling the man not to eavesdrop and threatening

Xenophobia against Muslim shoppers has also made news headlines since Trump entered office. But bigotry against Muslims in the US has risen since the 9/11 terror attacks.

him, she declared, "I ain't scared of no f-----g s--c. This is my f-----g country."[7]

The woman, later identified as Tiffany Cormier, lost her job in the American Airlines' payroll department as a result of her racist rant.[8] The public also learned that Cormier's husband is Latino, a fact that challenges the belief that someone can't be racist if they're in an interracial relationship.

Finally, at an Arkansas Walmart in May 2017, a white customer told a Mexican American shopper named Eva Hicks to "go back to wherever you're from."[9] The woman also told Hicks, "You're in America" and "This is not your country." When a Black customer told the woman not to be ignorant, she said, "A n----r is calling me ignorant?"

Hicks later said on Facebook that the racist encounter shocked her. "I never in my life thought this would happen to me," she wrote. "I love this country, and I will stay in this country."[10]

While Muslims and Latinxs have been among the most high-profile targets of this sort of harassment in stores, they are not alone. All people of color have been more vulnerable in today's political climate. An international student from Korea found this out in December 2017 at a California Starbucks. When the student, Annie An, and her tutor, Sean Lee, spoke Korean, a white woman told them, "Don't you dare say that again!" and "I don't want to hear the language."[11]

As the woman continued to harass them, Lee began filming her and later posted the footage to Facebook. He used the ordeal to educate the public about racism.

Following the 2016 presidential election, members of the Asian American and Latinx communities say racists have targeted them for speaking in any language other than English.

"In our day-to-day pursuits and responsibilities, it's all too easy to forget that racism and anti-immigrant sentiments are a real thing in this country, even in the Bay Area that so often touts 'diversity,'" he wrote.[12]

Dining Out

Racial minorities not only run into subtle racism while shopping or grabbing a coffee but also while dining out. In March 2018, a waitress asked a group of Black teens dining at a Maine IHOP to prepay for their meal. A white man who observed the encounter wrote about the incident in a Facebook post shared thousands of times. The man, Avery Gagne, said he and his parents confronted the waitress about her treatment of the teens.

She denied race played any role in her decision to ask the teens to prepay. Rather, that IHOP had a problem with teens dining and dashing, she said. But Gagne wrote on Facebook that the waitress immediately brought up the teens' race when explaining why she'd made them prepay.

A white man at a Maine IHOP stood up for a group of Black teens who were asked to pre-pay for their meal so they wouldn't dine and dash. By speaking out, the white diner proved himself to be a valuable ally.

The woman took it upon herself to make this group of teens pay for their meal upfront because she considered them 'high risk.' I don't care who has walked out on your establishment. That does not give you the right to determine who you believe is going to or not. My parents and I did not pay upfront for our meal, none of the tables around us prepaid for their meals. The fact that she stated 'it's not because of their color' proves it all.[13]

Gagne is a great example of how white allies can fight racism. He could've quietly kept eating his meal. Instead, he saw an injustice, responded to it, and let others know. Given that the teens were dining without guardians to help them respond to the situation, this was an honorable move on Gagne's part. But teens have power, too. If a business is treating you unfairly, you don't have to give them your hard-earned cash. You can ask to speak to a manager, write a letter to corporate headquarters, or post your complaint on social media.

Of course, not all microaggressions play out so openly in food establishments. The encounters some people of color have will be more subtle. In the second-season opener of Netflix's *One Day at a Time*, the Cuban-American Alvarez family chants in Spanish while dining at an ice cream parlor. A white patron soon approaches. "I know you're having a little *fiesta* over here, but you should really learn to keep your voice down," he tells them. "There are other people in here."[14]

Stunned into silence at first, single mom Penelope Alvarez decides to confront the man. She tells him that her family has just as much right to enjoy themselves as he does. She

One Day at a Time

Starring Rita Moreno and Justina Machado, *One Day at a Time* premiered in 2017 on Netflix. It is a remake of the 1975 sitcom of the same name. While the original focused on a white single mom raising two daughters in Indianapolis, Indiana, the remake chronicles a Cuban American single mom (Machado) in Los Angeles, California, raising a boy and a girl with the help of her mother (Moreno). The show tackles issues such as race, gender, sexual orientation, mental health, and veterans' rights.

In March 2018, Netflix announced it had renewed the show for a third season.[15]

The Netflix sitcom One Day at a Time *hasn't shied away from discussing serious topics like microaggressions. One episode showed the racial slights Latinx families may encounter while dining out.*

also picks up on the microaggression he used while hushing her family.

"I noticed you used the word 'fiesta,'" she says. "Would you care to comment on that?"

A direct confrontation is a great way to address microaggressions. Unfortunately, it may also be a risky move. You never know if a stranger will turn violent. Sometimes, you might want to confront a person. Other times, you'll want to ask store management to step in or to call for help. Trust your gut.

CHAPTER 5

Celebrities and Microaggressions

Behind the glitz and glamour, celebrities are people just like everyone else. They have family problems, health issues, and if they're Black or Brown, they've endured racial microaggressions. A number of famous people have discussed the impact of overt and covert racism on their lives. Learning their stories makes it clear just how far-reaching racism is. Even fame, fortune, and talent don't protect people of color from discrimination. But their accounts of racism show that attempts to make them feel inferior didn't stop them from following their dreams.

"Shut Up and Dribble"

Professional athletes have a long history of political activism. Most famously, Black boxer Muhammad Ali refused to serve in the Vietnam War in the 1960s. African Americans "are treated like dogs and denied simple human rights." he said.[1] At the 1968 Olympic Games in Mexico City, runners Tommie Smith and John Carlos used the award ceremony to protest racism and poverty. Smith had won the gold and Carlos the bronze medal in the 200-meter sprint. The two Black men removed their shoes to raise awareness about the poor and wore beads and scarves to call attention to lynching. For much of the twentieth century, racists killed people of color, often by hanging them. These acts of violence are known as lynchings.[2]

Smith and Carlos didn't just rely on accessories to make a political statement. When the US national anthem began to play during the ceremony, they raised their fists in what is known as the Black Power salute. Decades before Black Lives Matter came into being, these athletes wanted the world to

Muhammad Ali almost lost his boxing career when he refused to fight in the Vietnam War. In this photograph, Ali (right) points to a newspaper headline that shows he was far from the only protester against the war.

know the treatment Blacks faced in the United States was unacceptable. Journalists, activists, and historians continue to point out Smith and Carlos's bold gesture today.

Although athletes now live in a very different time, they continue to speak out about everything from microaggressions to police violence in communities of color. But some people would rather they stayed quiet. In February 2018, Fox News host Laura Ingraham said that Cleveland Cavaliers star LeBron James should "shut up and dribble" after he described some of Donald Trump's comments as "laughable and scary."[3]

Telling a basketball player to "shut up and dribble" is a microinvalidation. It ignores James's lived experience and dehumanizes him. As a Black man, James has certainly faced racism. In May 2017, for example, someone spray-painted racist graffiti on the gate of his Los Angeles home. He should be able to discuss his history with racism without others trying to silence him.

Ballerina Misty Copeland is a very different kind of athlete than LeBron James. But Copeland, who's Black, Italian, and German, has been open about racism and microaggressions in ballet. In 2015, she became the first Black woman to serve as a principal dancer for the prestigious American Ballet Theatre (ABT). She's used her influence to discuss the lack of racial diversity in the field.

Shortly before being named an ABT principal, she told British newspaper the *Telegraph* that ballet's racist history has affected her career. She explained how her looks have been questioned in a racialized way. She said:

Trailblazing ballerina Misty Copeland, who is multiracial, has been open about experiencing racism in the ballet world.

George Balanchine [the choreographer widely regarded as the father of American ballet] created this image of what a ballerina should be: skin the color of a peeled apple, with a prepubescent body... So when people think of ballet, that's what they expect to see, and when they see something different, it's 'wrong.'[4]

Copeland added that some people have said her (non-white) body isn't dancer material, that she shouldn't be in a tutu, and that she just doesn't "fit in." She's also faced microaggressions related to her hair. She recalled being told: "We shouldn't cast her because she probably can't get her hair in a classical 'do."

Of course, all ballerinas face scrutiny about how they look. But the idea that every ballerina should be the color of an apple's insides, have straight hair, and a European build sends a racist dog whistle. A dog whistle emits a pitch that dogs can hear but humans cannot. Yet a message has been sent all the same. In this case, no one is openly backing discrimination against Black and Brown dancers. But Balanchine's ideal ballerina is coded as white, and it's a code decision-makers know. To dancers of color who don't look like the ideal, the comments about their appearance present as microaggressions.

While athletes such as Misty Copeland and LeBron James have spoken out about racism without hurting their careers, this isn't true for every sports star. In 2016, then-San Francisco 49er Colin Kaepernick kneeled as the national anthem played during a game. Born to a white mother and Black father, he did so to call attention to police violence in communities of color. He went on to donate millions of dollars to charities and form a Know Your Rights camp for children.

For taking a knee during the national anthem, Kaepernick's career has suffered terribly. He became a free agent in March 2017, but a year later no NFL team had signed him. Many sports experts have blamed the NFL's disinterest in Kaepernick on his political views. No team has openly stated this, making their refusal to sign a qualified player a form of covert bias. A number of sports journalists agree that if Kaepernick had never taken a knee to show that Black lives mattered, he would still be playing in the NFL today. In fall 2017, Kaepernick filed a grievance against the NFL team owners for collusion—plotting to keep him from playing.[5]

But the football star has earned praise for speaking out against injustice. In 2017, *GQ* magazine named him its "citizen

Growing Up Kaepernick

Colin Kaepernick was born November 30, 1987, in Wisconsin to a teen mother. A white couple named Rick and Teresa Kaepernick adopted the biracial boy. They raised him in California.

Colin experienced microaggressions as the only Black child in his family. When they stayed in motels during summer trips, "the same thing always happened," he recalled in 2015. "Somebody would walk up to me, a real nervous manager, and say: 'Excuse me. Is there something I can help you with?'"[6]

The outside world treated Colin as if he didn't fit with his family, but he still had a close bond with them. Today, he receives many letters from adopted children. He's also traveled to Africa to learn more about his racial heritage.

Kaepernick remains unsigned after kneeling during the national anthem to raise awareness about police brutality.

of the year." His activism has inspired athletes from all ages and backgrounds to stand up for their beliefs.

Out of the Box

Meghan Markle, one of the newest members of the British royal family, grew up with a Black mom and white dad. From a very young age she faced microaggressions, she wrote in a 2015 *Elle* essay. She said that her freckles and light skin led strangers to assume her mother was her nanny, not her parent. This was a microinvalidation, as it ignored that biracial people come in a wide range of skin tones.

As Meghan grew up, she continued to face these sorts of microaggressions. For example, a teacher told her to check the "white" box on a school form that asked about her racial identity. The teacher explained this was because Meghan looked white. However, this was a microinvalidation that denied the reality of Meghan's Black heritage.

Throughout her life, Markle has often been asked "What are you?" or "Where are your parents from?" These questions make biracial people and other minorities feel singled out and different. No one should have to explain their racial background to strangers.

While attending Northwestern University, Markle continued to face subtle racism. She remembered the following exchange with a student who asked if her parents were still together.

> "You said your mom is Black and your dad is white, right?" she said. I smiled meekly, waiting for what could possibly come out of her pursed lips next. "And they're divorced?" I

Duchess of Sussex Meghan Markle, born to a Black mother and a white father, wrote an essay detailing her experiences with racial slights in childhood and adulthood alike.

nodded. "Oh, well that makes sense." To this day, I still don't fully understand what she meant by that, but I understood the implication.[7]

The student was suggesting that Blacks and whites don't belong in romantic relationships together, so of course Markle's parents had divorced. The remark is a microinsult, an insult that can be spoken or unspoken. These insults may not be delivered to intentionally cause harm, but what they suggest is hurtful.

During her college years, Markle experienced a microassault as well. While visiting her mother in Los Angeles, she witnessed a driver call her mother the N-word. Her mother's crime? Not pulling out of a parking space quickly enough for the driver.

Markle is far from the only entertainer to suffer microaggressions. The Black actress and singer Jennifer Hudson told *Cosmopolitan* magazine in 2018 that when she takes planes, the flight attendants assume that she doesn't belong in first class. She also described how people assume that her home belongs to her white driver and not to her.[8]

Oprah Winfrey is one of the richest women on the planet, but while shopping in Switzerland in 2013, a store clerk refused to show her a luxury handbag. The clerk told her it was "too expensive." Sure, the purse cost $38,000, but for a billionaire like Winfrey, the price tag wasn't a problem.[9]

The Indian American actress Mindy Kaling, Winfrey's *Wrinkle in Time* costar, is well known for sitcom *The Mindy Project*. But when Kaling attended the 2014 New Yorker Festival after-party, she said an elderly white man began praising her. Before long, Kaling realized the man had mistaken her for Malala Yousafzai, the Nobel Peace Prize winner from Pakistan. Yousafzai is a girls' education activist, gunned down in 2012 by a member of political group the Taliban. By confusing Kaling for Malala, the man sent the message that all Brown people look alike. After all, Kaling was thirty-five at the time, and Malala was just seventeen. The two are both of South Asian origin but do not resemble each other.

Oprah Winfrey may be one of the richest people in the world, but even she's dealt with the perception that she couldn't afford to buy expensive items in stores.

Ever the comedienne, Kaling laughed off the micro-aggression. "Did he really think I'm Malala?" she wondered. "And that if I were, I'd be at the Boom Boom Room [bar]?" [10]

Sometimes, racism can be so ridiculous that you may feel like "laughing to keep from crying." Other times you may need to cry. On occasion, you may feel like fighting back. Fighting

Actress Mindy Kaling (right) was confused for girls' education advocate Malala Yousafzai (left) at a party, despite their significant age difference and difference in appearance.

back doesn't mean a violent confrontation. It can mean participating in political activism, speaking out about your experiences, or pouring them into writing or art. It can mean speaking to a counselor about how racism has affected you. Simply put, it means protecting yourself from harm.

CHAPTER 6

Protecting Yourself

"Self-care" is a term that's thrown around a lot these days. It's been used to describe everything from pampering oneself to enjoying a night out with friends. But at its core, self-care means putting one's mental and physical health first. When applied to covert and overt racism, it can mean avoiding racists, confronting racists, or valuing yourself in a world bent on devaluing you. One way to value yourself is to let out your feelings about the mistreatment you've endured because of your skin color.

Let It Out

If you're dealing with any form of racism, one of the best ways to respond is to discuss what you're going through. Some people like to pretend that bigotry doesn't exist. But behaving this way hurts people of color. A 2010 study on Filipino Americans and racism found that women who ignored subtle racism suffered more stress

A Filipino American History Month event in Los Angeles, 2016. A study of Filipino Americans showed they have better mental health when they discuss microaggressions instead of ignoring them.

than those who did not keep quiet about it. Those who spoke up or confronted those to blame even felt more self-esteem.[1] That's right. Discussing racism may actually be good for you.

The next time you experience a microaggression, talk it out. Tell people you can trust about what happened. If you feel like it's safe to confront the person who targeted you with such behavior, do so. You can point out why you found the person's actions or words offensive. Just remember that you can't make someone admit to wrongdoing. The person may deny, deny, deny, but you can take pride in the fact that you stood up for yourself.

Sometimes you might not feel like confronting the person who behaved badly. Honor your feelings. If you prefer, listen to music, write in your journal, or watch a funny movie to lift your spirits. You have no obligation to further expose yourself to a harmful individual. If you have any inkling that the individual may turn violent, walk away. Your safety is more important than trying to help bigots see why their behavior is unacceptable.

You can also "let it out" by writing poetry, creating art, or writing a whole book about your experiences. President Barack Obama did just that when he published *Dreams from My Father* in 1995. At the time he wasn't famous, or even a politician. Yet, he poured his heart into a book about his life experiences. He wrote about growing up without his Black father, his white family members, school life, and first visit to Kenya.

Once Obama became president, racists exposed him to an entirely new level of racism. They made racist cartoons, likening him to chimpanzees, and spread rumors that he was a terrorist. First Lady Michelle Obama received similar treatment. She discussed this while speaking to the graduating class of Tuskegee University in 2015. She said:

> It knocked me back a bit. It made me wonder, just how are people seeing me. All of this used to really get to me. Back in those days, I had a lot of sleepless nights, worrying about what people thought of me, wondering if I might be hurting my husband's chances of winning his election, fearing how my girls would feel if they found out what some people were saying about their mom.[2]

Born in Hawaii to a Black Kenyan father and a white Kansan mother, Barack Obama explored his racial identity in his 1995 memoir, **Dreams from My Father.**

Michelle Obama was brave enough to make public the effect that racial microaggressions had on her. Discussing the pain of racism is in no way shameful.

It's not just the Obamas who have channeled their experiences with subtle racism into books and speeches. Indian American comedian Hari Kondabolu made a whole documentary about the teasing and taunts he suffered as a child because of the stereotypical portrayal of *Simpsons* character Apu Nahasapeemapetilon, an Indian American.

Girl of the South Side[3]

Michelle Obama was born January 17, 1964, in Chicago, Illinois. Her father, Fraser Robinson, worked for the city water plant. Her mother, Marian Robinson, worked as a secretary and homemaker.[4]

Michelle was a good student, skipping second grade. She attended Whitney Young Magnet High School on Chicago's South Side. From there, she went to Princeton University, where she received a bachelor's degree in sociology. She attended Harvard for law school.

She met Barack Obama at a Chicago law firm. They married in 1992. Their children, Malia and Sasha, arrived in 1998 and 2001.

Michelle Obama has worked in public service and for Chicago hospitals. In 2009, she became the forty-fourth First Lady, a role she used to champion healthful eating, exercise, and military families.

First Lady Michelle Obama grew up in a working-class household on Chicago's South Side. She's told students how important it is not to let racial stereotypes define them.

Voiced by a white actor, Apu is a convenience store owner who repeatedly delivers the line, "Thank you, come again."

In his documentary, *The Problem with Apu*,[5] Kondabolu describes why the character was a stereotype and how his classmates used Apu to torment him as a child. He also interviewed other Indian Americans with similar experiences. None of them felt that Apu accurately represented Indian immigrants they knew. This makes the cartoon character (created by whites) a microinvalidation and a stereotype.

Fighting Back

Sometimes a racial microaggression will feel like such an injustice that you'll want to take action. In 2015, school

Hari Kondabolu, director of **The Problem with Apu,** *poses with actress Whoopi Goldberg, who appears in the film about the stereotypical character from* **The Simpsons.**

officials told the parents of a seven-year-old Seneca boy named Jakobe that he could not wear his Mohawk hairstyle to school. They said the cut distracted his classmates. But the hairstyle is part of traditional Seneca culture. Calling it a distraction and asking the parents to cut the boy's hair invalidated their culture.

The boy's father, Gary Sanden, refused to do as told. "I told the superintendent I was [by] no means going to cut his hair because it's a symbol of who we are," he said.[6]

The family presented a letter from their tribe to the school district explaining the role of Mohawks in Seneca culture. The little boy was ultimately allowed to wear his Mohawk to school. His parents stood up for him and their culture and won.

It can feel intimidating to challenge officials at a school, workplace, or business. But if these officials are in the wrong, you have the right to fight back. Write letters, complain to a supervisor, plan a protest. Do what you believe is necessary to fight against injustice.

Supporters, or allies, of the oppressed can fight back, too. In April 2018, staff at a Philadelphia Starbucks called the police on two Black men simply for being in the coffee shop without ordering.[7] They were waiting on a friend to show up, but the staff said they were trespassing and called the cops to remove them. When police arrived, witnesses at the coffee shop intervened. They acted as allies, telling the authorities that the men had done nothing wrong. One ally recorded the incident and posted it to Twitter. The video went

Racial bias training—like what Starbucks organized in eight thousand stores after the arrest of two Black men for not ordering immediately—can be a helpful way to ease racial microaggressions in our society.

viral and before long, concerned citizens were calling for a Starbucks boycott.

Allies are important because ending racism isn't the responsibility of the oppressed. It's the responsibility of everyone in society, especially those who have the most privilege. If you see an act of racism, take the time to do something. It may not always be safe to immediately confront the people involved. However, you may be able to ask questions, record the incident, share what happened on social media, or alert the news media. Let the victims of racial microaggressions know that you care.

Chapter Notes

Chapter 1
Just What Are Microaggressions?

1. Tori DeAngelis, "Unmasking 'Racial Micro Aggressions,'" *Monitor on Psychology*, February 2009, http://www.apa.org/monitor/2009/02/microaggression.aspx.
2. Ibid.
3. Ibid.
4. D.W. Sue, C.M. Capodilupo, G.C. Torino, J.M. Bucceri, A.M.B. Holder, K.L. Nadal, and M. Esquilin, "Racial Microaggressions in Everyday Life," *American Psychologist*, May/June 2007.
5. Derald Wing Sue, "Racial Microaggressions in Everyday Life: Is Subtle Bias Harmless?", *Psychology Today*, October 5, 2010, https://www.psychologytoday.com/blog/microaggressions-in-everyday-life/201010/racial-microaggressions-in-everyday-life.
6. "Dr. Chester Pierce," MGH Division of Global Psychiatry, retrieved March 8, 2018, http://www.mghglobalpsychiatry.org/chesterpierce.php.
7. Ibid.
8. Sue, "Racial Microaggressions in Everyday Life."
9. Ibid.
10. DeAngelis, "Unmasking 'Racial Micro Aggressions.'"
11. Tanzina Vega, "Students See Many Slights as Racial 'Microaggressions,'" *New York Times*, March 21, 2014, https://www.nytimes.com/2014/03/22/us/as-diversity-increases-slights-get-subtler-but-still-sting.html.

Chapter 2
Why Microaggressions Matter

1. "Transcript of George Zimmerman's Call to the Police," Archive.org, retrieved March 11, 2018, https://archive.org/stream/326700-full-transcript-zimmerman/326700-full-transcript-zimmerman_djvu.txt.
2. Ibid.
3. Alexander Abad-Santos, "Watch: Trayvon Martin Buying Skittles and Iced Tea at 7-Eleven," *Atlantic*, May 18, 2012, https://www.theatlantic.com/national/archive/2012/05/watch-trayvon-martin-buying-skittles-and-iced-tea-7-eleven/327947.
4. Greg Botelho and Holly Yan, "George Zimmerman Found Not Guilty of Murder in Trayvon Martin's Death," CNN.com, July 14, 2013, https://www.cnn.com/2013/07/13/justice/zimmerman-trial/index.html.
5. David Ovalle, "Miami Judge Rules Florida's New Stand-Your-Ground Law Is Unconstitutional," *Miami Herald*, July 3, 2017, http://www.miamiherald.com/news/local/crime/article159394094.html.

6. Travis M. Andrews, "George Zimmerman's Many, Many Controversies Since the Trayvon Martin Case," *Chicago Tribune*, May 12, 2016, http://www.chicagotribune.com/news/nationworld/ct-george-zimmerman-controversies-20160512-story.html.
7. Audra D.S. Burch and Laura Isensee, "Trayvon Martin, a Typical Teen with Dreams of Flying or Fixing Planes," *Tampa Bay Times*, March 23, 2012, http://www.tampabay.com/news/publicsafety/crime/trayvon-martin-a-typical-teen-with-dreams-of-flying-or-fixing-planes/1221425.
8. Ibid.
9. Patrisse Cullors, "On Trayvon Martin's Birthday, We Remember His Life and Why We Fight for Black Lives," NBCNews.com, February 5, 2018, https://www.nbcnews.com/think/opinion/trayvon-martin-s-birthday-we-remember-his-life-why-we-ncna844711.
10. Stanford Medicine News Center, "Infants' Race Influences Quality of Hospital Care in California," August 27, 2017, Med.Stanford.edu, https://med.stanford.edu/news/all-news/2017/08/infants-race-influences-quality-of-hospital-care-in-california.html.
11. Nadra Kareem Nittle, "Why Racism in Health Care Is Still a Problem Today," Thoughtco.com, updated March 18, 2017, https://www.thoughtco.com/racism-in-health-care-still-a-problem-2834530.
12. APA Staff, "Racism and Mental Health," American Psychiatric Association, October 6, 2017, https://www.psychiatry.org/news-room/apa-blogs/apa-blog/2017/10/racism-and-mental-health.

Chapter 3

The Soft Bigotry of Low Expectations

1. The White House, Office of the Press Secretary, "Remarks by the President at Morehouse College Commencement Ceremony," The White House: President Barack Obama, May 19, 2013, https://obamawhitehouse.archives.gov/the-press-office/2013/05/19/remarks-president-morehouse-college-commencement-ceremony.
2. Rasheed Malik, "New Data Reveal 250 Preschoolers Are Suspended or Expelled Every Day," Center for American Progress, November 6, 2017, https://www.americanprogress.org/issues/early-childhood/news/2017/11/06/442280/new-data-reveal-250-preschoolers-suspended-expelled-every-day.
3. Ibid.
4. Ibid.
5. US Department of Education, "School Climate and Discipline: Know the Data," Ed.gov, retrieved March 18, 2018, https://www2.ed.gov/policy/gen/guid/school-discipline/data.html.

6. Teresa Watanabe, "L.A. Unified bans suspension for 'willful defiance,'" *Los Angeles Times,* http://articles.latimes.com/2013/may/14/local/la-me-lausd-suspension-20130515.
7. Association for Psychological Science, "Faces of Black Children as Young as Five Evoke Negative Biases," PsychologicalScience.org, February 8, 2016, https://www.psychologicalscience.org/news/releases/faces-of-black-children-as-young-as-five-evoke-negative-biases.html.
8. Olivia Goldhill, "The World Is Relying on a Flawed Psychological Test to Fight Racism," Quartz.com, December 3, 2017, https://qz.com/1144504/the-world-is-relying-on-a-flawed-psychological-test-to-fight-racism.
9. Jason A. Grissom and Christopher Redding, "Discretion and Disproportionality: Explaining the Underrepresentation of High-Achieving Students of Color in Gifted Programs," January 19, 2016, http://www.aera.net/Newsroom/News-Releases-and-Statements/Does-Student-Race-Affect-Gifted-Assignment/Discretion-and-Disproportionality-Explaining-the-Underrepresentation-of-High-Achieving-Students-of-Color-in-Gifted-Programs.
10. Susan Dynarski, "Why Talented Black and Hispanic Students Can Go Undiscovered," *New York Times*, April 8, 2016, https://www.nytimes.com/2016/04/10/upshot/why-talented-black-and-hispanic-students-can-go-undiscovered.html?emc=eta1&_r=0.
11. "Excerpts from Bush's Speech on Improving Education," *New York Times*, September 3, 1999, http://www.nytimes.com/1999/09/03/us/excerpts-from-bush-s-speech-on-improving-education.html.
12. Jeremy Bauer-Wolf, "A September of Racist Incidents," *Inside Higher Ed*, September 22, 2017, https://www.insidehighered.com/news/2017/09/22/racist-incidents-colleges-abound-academic-year-begins.
13. Associated Press, "Police: Connecticut College Student Put Body Fluids on Roommate's Belongings," *Chicago Tribune*, November 1, 2017, http://www.chicagotribune.com/news/nationworld/ct-college-student-body-fluids-tampering-20171101-story.html.
14. Anemona Hartocollis, "Long After Protests, Students Shun the University of Missouri," *New York Times*, July 9, 2017, https://www.nytimes.com/2017/07/09/us/university-of-missouri-enrollment-protests-fallout.html?mtrref=www.google.com.
15. Kate Parkinson-Morgan, "Alexandra Wallace Apologizes, Announces She Will No Longer Attend UCLA," *Daily Bruin*, March 18, 2011, https://dailybruin.com/2011/03/18/alexandra_wallace_apologizes_announces_she_will_no_longer_attend_ucla.

Chapter 4

Shopping While Black (or Brown)

1. James Conley III, "Today I was racially profiled by the Old Navy store in West Des Moines, Iowa," Facebook.com, January 30, 2018, https://www.facebook.com/james.i.conley.9/posts/10157042735500898.
2. Rachel Herron, "Old Navy Fired the Three Employees Who Accused a Black Customer of Stealing His Own Jacket," BET.com, February 5, 2018, https://www.bet.com/news/national/2018/02/05/old-navy-fired-the-three-employees-who-accused-a-black-customer-.html.
3. Frank Newport, "Despite Unrest, Blacks Do Not Feel More Mistreated by Police," Gallup.com, August 3, 2015, http://news.gallup.com/poll/184439/despite-unrest-blacks-feel-mistreated-police.aspx.
4. Mandy Velez, "Woman Tells Latina Customers to 'Speak English' in Racist Rant at Kentucky JCPenney Store," *Independent*, December 21, 2016, https://www.independent.co.uk/news/world/americas/louisville-racist-rant-video-kentucky-jcpenney-mall-woman-two-latinas-speak-english-a7489391.html.
5. Ibid.
6. Staff, "Woman Allegedly Harasses Muslim Shopper at Trader Joe's," Fox5DC.com, May 7, 2017, http://www.fox5dc.com/news/trending/woman-allegedly-harasses-muslim-shopper-at-trader-joes.
7. Breanna Edwards, "Woman Goes on Racist Rant in Manassas, Va., Store, Calls Latino Man a 'S--c,'" TheRoot.com, May 23, 2017, https://www.theroot.com/woman-goes-on-racist-rant-in-manassas-va-store-calls-1795454557.
8. Ibid.
9. Thatiana Diaz, "Walmart Shopper Tells Latina Woman to 'Go Back to Mexico,'" *People*, May 24, 2017, http://people.com/chica/walmart-shopper-tells-latina-woman-to-go-back-to-mexico.
10. Ibid.
11. Rafi Schwartz, "White Lady Hauled Away by Cops After Racist Freakout at Korean Woman at Bay Area Starbucks," SplinterNews.com, December 14, 2017, https://splinternews.com/white-lady-hauled-away-by-cops-after-racist-freakout-at-1821286342.
12. Ibid.
13. Doug Criss, "A Waitress Asked Some Black Teens to Prepay for Their Meal. A Fellow Diner Wasn't Having That," CNN.com, March 16, 2018, https://www.cnn.com/2018/03/15/us/maine-ihop-race-trnd/index.html.
14. Gloria Calderon Kellett and Mike Royce, *One Day at a Time*, streaming television, directed by Pamela Fryman, (2018; Los Angeles, CA: Netflix).

15. Joe Otterson, "One Day at a Time' Renewed for Season 3 at Netflix," *Variety*, March 26, 2018, http://variety.com/2018/tv/news/one-day-at-a-time-renewed-season-3-netflix-1202736288.

Chapter 5
Celebrities and Microaggressions

1. "Muhammad Ali Inspirational Quotes on Success and Racism," AlJazeera.com, January 18, 2018, https://www.aljazeera.com/news/2016/06/muhammad-ali-life-quotes-160604094217123.html.
2. DeNeen L. Brown, "They didn't #TakeTheKnee: The Black Power Protest Salute That Shook the World in 1968," *Washington Post*, September 24 2017, https://www.washingtonpost.com/news/retropolis/wp/2017/09/24/they-didnt-takeaknee-the-black-power-protest-salute-that-shook-the-world-in 1968/?utm_term=.4cfef31c36ad.
3. Emily Sullivan, "Laura Ingraham Told LeBron James to Shut Up and Dribble; He Went to the Hoop," NPR.org, February 19, 2018, https://www.npr.org/sections/thetwo-way/2018/02/19/587097707/laura-ingraham-told-lebron-james-to-shutup-and-dribble-he-went-to-the-hoop.
4. James Mulkerrins, "Misty Copeland: meet the ballerina who rewrote the rules of colour, class and curves," *Telegraph*, June 21, 2015, https://www.telegraph.co.uk/culture/theatre/dance/11675707/Misty-Copeland-ballerina-interview.html.
5. Jeff Zrebeic, "Ravens' Newsome, Harbaugh Will Be Questioned Under Oath in Kaepernick Grievance, Per Report," *Baltimore Sun*, April 4, 2018, http://www.baltimoresun.com/sports/ravens/ravens-insider/bs-sp-newsome-harbaugh-kaepernick-20180404-story.html.
6. Andrew Corsello, "Mr. Colin Kaepernick," *Mr. Porter*, retrieved April 5, 2018, https://www.mrporter.com/journal/the-look/mr-colin-kaepernick/535.
7. Meghan Markle, "I'm More Than an 'Other,'" *Elle*, July 2015, https://www.elle.com/uk/life-and-culture/news/a26855/more-than-an-other.
8. Daniella Scott, "Jennifer Hudson Gets Real About Prejudice and Women Taking a Stand," *Cosmopolitan*, January 4, 2018, https://www.cosmopolitan.com/uk/entertainment/a14538833/jennifer-hudson-racism-prejudice-weinstein.
9. Nick Thompson and Diana Magnay, "Oprah Winfrey Racism Row Over Switzerland Shop Incident," CNN.com, August 11, 2013, https://www.cnn.com/2013/08/09/world/oprah-winfrey-racism-switzerland/index.html.
10. Jacob Bernstein, "Mindy Kaling Hasn't Won a Nobel Prize. Yet." *New York Times*, October 24, 2014, https://www.nytimes.com/2014/10/26/fashion/

mindy-kaling-talks-at-the-new-yorker-festival.html?smid=nytcore-iphone-share&smprod=nytcore-iphone&_r=2.

Chapter 6

Protecting Yourself

1. Alvin N. Alvarez and Linda Juang, "Filipino Americans and Racism: A Multiple Mediation Model of Coping," *Journal of Counseling Psychology*, April 2010, https://www.researchgate.net/publication/49660174_Filipino_Americans_and_Racism_A_Multiple_Mediation_Model_of_Coping.
2. Britni Danielle, "Michelle Obama's 'Twice As Good' Speech Doesn't Cut It with Most African Americans," *Guardian*, May 12, 2015, https://www.theguardian.com/commentisfree/2015/may/12/michelle-obama-twice-as-good-african-americans-black-people.
3. Kenzie Bryant, "President Obama's Tribute to Michelle Brought Malia to Tears," *Vanity Fair*, January 10, 2017, https://www.vanityfair.com/style/2017/01/barack-obama-farewell-speech-michelle-sasha-malia-tribute.
4. "Michelle Obama Biography," Biography.com, retrieved April 14, 2018, https://www.biography.com/people/michelle-obama-307592.
5. Hari Kondabolu, *The Problem with Apu*, television, directed by Michael Melamedoff (2017; Atlanta, GA.: TruTV).
6. Lindsey Bever, "Native American Boy Pulled from Class Over Mohawk Haircut," *Washington Post*, September 19, 2015, https://www.washingtonpost.com/news/morning-mix/wp/2015/09/19/native-american-boy-pulled-from-class-over-mohawk-haircut/?noredirect=on&utm_term=.9cf902d270dc.
7. Emily Stewart, "Two Black Men Were Arrested in a Philadelphia Starbucks for Doing Nothing," Vox.com, April 14, 2018, https://www.vox.com/identities/2018/4/14/17238494/what-happened-at-starbucks-black-men-arrested-philadelphia.

Glossary

ally A friend or supporter; a country that takes the same side as another in a political conflict.

bias Prejudice against a certain group, especially involving race or gender.

concept An idea, model, or design.

covert Describing behavior or activity that is done in secret or not in the open, often on purpose.

discrimination The act of treating one person or group differently from others, often because of race, gender, nationality, etc.

indignity Shameful or humiliating treatment of a person or group, leading to a loss of respect or pride.

Jim Crow The group of laws that kept Blacks and whites apart, or segregated, from each other in the American South.

mental health One's emotional or psychological well-being.

oppression Keeping a certain group down or denying the group rights or equal treatment in a system, government, or country.

overt Describing behavior or activity that is done openly and obviously.

privilege An edge or advantage in society because of wealth, skin color, gender, ability, etc.

psychiatry The field of medicine that focuses on the mind and its health.

racism The belief that one racial group is superior to another, and the system that works to keep racial inequality in place.

stereotype A belief that unfairly groups together people of a certain race, ethnicity, gender, class, etc., as all the same.

xenophobia The fear or hatred of foreigners.

Further Reading

Books

Copeland, Misty. *Life in Motion: An Unlikely Ballerina.* New York, NY: Touchstone Books, 2014.

Fulton, Sybrina, and Tracy Martin. *Rest in Power: The Enduring Life of Trayvon Martin.* New York, NY: Spiegel & Grau, 2017.

Krajnik, Elizabeth. *Meghan Markle: American Royal.* New York, NY: Enslow, 2018.

Oluo, Ijeoma. *So You Want to Talk About Race.* New York, NY: Seal Press, 2018.

Websites

Asian Americans Advancing Justice

www.advancingjustice-aajc.org

A civil and human rights organization for Asian Americans.

National Museum of African American History and Culture

nmaahc.si.edu

This museum includes exhibits, collections, videos, and information about Blacks in the United States.

Presente

presente.org

An online Latinx organization that promotes social justice through technology, media, and culture.

Teaching Tolerance

www.tolerance.org

A project of the Southern Poverty Law Center, Teaching Tolerance provides educational materials about diversity and justice.

Index